The Diabetic Diet

Recipes for Type 2 Diabetes

William A. Clark

Contents

1. Introduction   1

2. What Causes Diabetes   9

3. Beef Curry that is Simple to Make   33

4. Chile Relleno Casserole with Salsa Salad   48

5. Lime Zinger Dressing   68

6. Conclusion   77

Chapter One

Introduction

A year prior, I was determined to have Type 2 diabetes. I was overweight and an absolute sugar and carb fiend. The specialist let me know that I would should be taking drugs and need to live with this infection for the remainder of my life. I watched my dad experience the ill effects of diabetes. I saw him infuse insulin consistently and I would rather not end up like him. I was concerned and became fixated on tracking down a fix. So I did my examination. I saw numerous recordings and read many books on diabetes, however none of these recordings and books gave a basic and clear way to deal with overseeing diabetes. Because of the absence of straightforward materials in dealing with the circumstance, I did a colossal measure of exploration and an acknowledged food the board, solid living, and exercise are the main elements in type 2 diabetics management.

2 THE DIABETIC DIET

My basic Type 2 diabetes the executives technique gave me trust. By then, I subscribed to a severe eating routine. I did this diet as if my life depended on it. I ate less carbs a day and kept away from sugar. I checked my glucose level something like six times each day to get a total image of how everything treated my blood glucose levels. Following a month and a half, my glucose was ideal for a non-diabetic. No medication. Simply diet and exercise. It has now been around ten months. I presently do a moderate carb and fat eating regimen. Very little red meat. Fish, chicken, bunches of veggies and mixed greens with oil and vinegar, cheeses, and entire grain bread. During winter and I eat pasta, some pizza, and bounty natural product. No sugars. Every so often, I eat chocolate. I check my blood glucose levels each prior day breakfast. My blood glucose level never surpasses 5.6 (100). It ordinarily goes from 4.3 to 5.2, regardless of whether I have pasta or pizza at supper. I put forth a valiant effort to live with as little pressure as could really be expected and have a quality sleep.

By following this way of life that was broadly based on sound diet the board, I had the option to invert diabetes. I'm in good company in this. There are huge number of individuals who have comparative stories. Certain individuals earnestly accept that Type 2 diabetes is an irreversible and moderate illness. They are just rehashing everything that they have been said by the drug and clinical businesses who have a monetary interest in not restoring diabetes. I'm propelled to compose this book as a result of you. The 200 plans, 21-day dinner plan in this cookbook are new options that proposition trust and have incredibly assisted me with dealing with my diabetes, and I accept it will extraordinarily help you too.

Some individuals are brought into the world with diabetes; notwithstanding, a huge number of individuals are determined to have Type 2 diabetes consistently in any case called grown-up beginning diabetes. Upon analysis, assuming you're similar to me, you are probably going to be disturbed, confounded, and uncertain of where to go. This basic cookbook is intended to assist recently determined Type 2 diabetics patients to have slipping into another eating regimen and method of living.

When you 're determined to have Type 2 diabetes, blood glucose levels are a consistent concern. Notwithstanding, with the appropriate eating schedule, you wouldn't need to stress. We as a whole love delicious food; great meatloaf, velvety macintosh, and cheddar or healthy spaghetti with meatballs. Sadly, many individuals accept that a diabetes determination implies they can't partake in these scrumptious food varieties. Actually, it just takes a few additional consideration

with fixings and a few minor acclimations to plans to refresh these delicious food sources for a lowglycemic diet.

This broad cookbook of diabetes-accommodating plans is planned with adoration to be impeccably distributed for individuals with Type 2 diabetes. Whether or not you're attempting to thwart or control diabetes, your nourishing prerequisites are practically equivalent to everybody's. In any case, you really do need to zero in on a few eating regimen decisions, particularly starches. While practicing and living sound can help, the main thing you can do is practice good eating habits. Practicing good eating habits can assist you with losing a huge level of your complete weight, lower pulse, glucose, and cholesterol levels. Eating better can moreover altogether affect temperament, energy, and feeling of well-being.

Getting determined to have diabetes can be unnerving, especially in the event that you have no clue about the following stages to take. You may begin to ask yourself, "Should I be on medicine and supplements? Should I enroll in an exercise program? Should I do this? Should I do that?" These are the thoughts that will run through your mind, and these cycles can be overpowering. In any case, the main choice that I made was changing my eating routine arrangement. Food is an essential piece of our endurance, and we love to eat. For a person with diabetes, this doesn't have to change. You don't have to relinquish nourishment for diabetes.

Notwithstanding, presenting yourself to new plans and supper thoughts is never something terrible. You ought to just change your prediabetes top choices into better food choices. The flavor shouldn't be an issue since there are multiple ways you can expand your dinners to keep them great yet healthier.

It 's critical for people with diabetes to screen their weight control plans eagerly, as the sickness extraordinarily builds one's danger of respiratory failure or stroke. This far reaching cookbook incorporates tidbits and dessert and doesn't relinquish taste for sound slimming down. Some of the time, we as a whole need for snacks, correct? For most individuals, dinner arranging is testing and will in general be significantly more trying for diabetic patients. This cookbook suggests individuals with diabetes fill their supper plates with veggies, protein, starch, or grain. Every one of the plans in the book keep guideline essential parceling, permitting you to blend various parts of different eating regimen as you wish. This clear methodology makes the most common way of building solid and delectable dinners simpler.

The general goal of this book is to give desire to Type 2 diabetes patients by assisting them with dealing with their condition through the arrangement of fundamental data, key abilities, assets, and backing expected to accomplish ideal wellbeing. Here is a book that responds to the genuine inquiry regarding Type 2 diabetes. This book is for as of late determined people to have Type 2 diabetes or anybody prepared to control their dietary patterns. Type 2 diabetics cookbook for amateurs is a complete, bit by bit presentation for individuals with type 2 diabetes. This book guides you through your diabetic excursion, empowering you to settle on sound eating regimen decisions at every turn. This book contains a 21-Day flavorful and good feast plan that upholds the personal satisfaction for individuals with Type 2 diabetes through diet plans while further developing the individual's very own feeling of control and well-being.

The straightforward plans utilized in this book maintain the physiological wellbeing of individuals with type 2 diabetes by keeping up with blood glucose as close to typical as could be expected. Diabetes is preventable and can even be switched. Assuming that you're as of now

determined to have type 2 diabetes, it's never past the time to roll out a positive improvement by eating better, working out, and carrying on with a sound way of life. Overseeing diabetes through diet doesn't mean living in hardship; it implies eating a tasty, adjusted eating regimen that will further develop your mind-set and lift your energy. You don't surrender to a long period of bland food. This book contains a few fantastic diabetic weight control plans, with a lot of scrumptious suppers that wouldn't set your glucose taking off, helping you arranged to carry on with a glad and all around fed life notwithstanding being a diabetic.

What Is Diabetes?

Diabetes is one of the main sources of unexpected passing in the United States. As per records, around 1.4 million new instances of diabetes are analyzed every year, and an expected 8 million individuals are undiscovered or ignorant of their condition. The assessed number of individuals over 18 determined and undiscovered to have diabetes is over 30.2 million. Diabetes is a problem where the body doesn't involve the sugars in food in a normal way. The side effects of diabetes in individuals contrast, contingent upon the degree and intricacy of the confusion. At the point when the body can't get sugar at the necessary spot and time, it prompts raised glucose levels in the circulatory framework, prompting intricacies like nerve, kidney, eye, and cardiovascular disease.

Sugar (glucose) is the most favored fuel for synapses and muscle. Be that as it may, it expects insulin to ship the glucose into cells for use. But when insulin levels are low, this means the insulin isn't sufficient to transport the sugar into the cells. This interaction prompts raised glucose levels. After a long enough time-line, the cells foster insulin obstruction, and the consideration presently changes to the pancreas, which is needed to make more insulin to move sugar into the cells; regardless, more sugar is still left in the blood. Because of the strain on the pancreas, it will ultimately "wears out," and that implies it will never again emit sufficient insulin to move the sugar into the cells for energy.

8   THE DIABETIC DIET

Without ceaseless and cautious administration, diabetes can prompt perilous entanglements, including visual deficiency and foot removals, heart or kidney sickness. It can prompt the improvement of sugars in the blood, expanding the danger of perilous unexpected problems, including stroke and heart disease.

Chapter Two

What Causes Diabetes

The quantity of instances of Type 2 diabetes is taking off, connected with the corpulence scourge. Type 2 diabetes happens over the long run and includes issues getting sufficient sugar (glucose) into the body's cells. Overweight or stout is the most serious danger factor for Type 2 diabetes. In any case, the danger is higher in the event that the grouping of weight is around the midsection instead of the thighs and hips. The paunch fat that encompasses the liver and stomach organs are firmly connected to insulin obstruction. Calories obtained from everyday sugary drinks such as energy drinks, soda, coffee drinks, and processed foods like muffins, doughnuts, cereal, and candy could greatly increase the weight around your abdomen. As well as practicing good eating habits, scaling back sweet food varieties can mean a slimmer waistline just as a lower hazard of diabetes.

Symptoms of Type 1&2 Diabetes include:

Coma Itching Hunger Confusion Chest pain Headaches Blurry vision

Extreme thirst Increased urination Fatigue or weakness Problems with gums

Unexplained weight loss Problems having an erection Nausea, diarrhea, or constipation Numbness in the hands and feet

Diabetes is an inconvenient illness to live with, paying little heed to how experienced you are.

Grown-ups determined to have Type 2 diabetes might have difficulties choosing what to eat and what not to eat. Without a doubt, even the individuals who have lived with diabetes for a long while could generally utilize additional direction and great abstaining from excessive food intake advice.

Differences Between Type 1 and Type 2 Diabetes

Most individuals realize there are two sorts of diabetes, yet not every person comprehends the contrast between them. The principle contrast between the two sorts of diabetes is that type 1 diabetes, otherwise called insulinsubordinate diabetes, is an immune system problem that regularly starts in adolescence. It is a condition wherein the resistant framework is assaulting and annihilating the insulin-creating cells in your pancreas, or the pancreas cells are not working viably, prompting a decrease in the development of insulin. Without insulin, the glucose from starch food varieties can't enter the cells. This makes glucose develop in the blood, leaving your body's cells and tissues starved for energy.

Type 2, otherwise called grown-up beginning diabetes, is the most widely recognized type of diabetes. Type 2 diabetes is generally diet-related and can be brought about by various elements. One component that might cause this kind of diabetes is the point at which the pancreas starts to make less insulin. The subsequent conceivable reason impervious to insulin. This implies could be that the body the pancreas is delivering becomes

insulin, however the body doesn't utilize it effectively. In both sort 1 and type 2 diabetes, glucose levels can get too high in light of the fact that the body doesn't create insulin or it doesn't use insulin appropriately. Diabetes can be made due, and diabetics patients can in any case carry on with a generally "ordinary" life.

How to Prevent Diabetes and Control Sugar Level

Because type 1 diabetes is nonexclusive, blood tests are vital for analysis. Nonetheless, blood tests that decide the probability of type 1 must be suggested by specialists when a patient starts to show manifestations. An A1C screening tests the glucose levels between a few months and is commonly used to analyze type 1 and type 2 diabetes. Dissimilar to type 1 diabetes which is conventional, there are numerous ways of forestalling type 2 diabetes. Ways of forestalling type 2 diabetes include:

Healthy diet Quit smoking

Increase your fiber intake

Exercise and weight management Maintain average blood pressure Maintain low alcohol consumption

Treatment for Diabetes Type 1 diabetes has no fix; in any case, it very well may be overseen by infusing insulin into the greasy tissue under the skin. The objective of Type 1 diabetic administration is to keep up with solid blood glucose levels when dinners. The patient necessities to comprehend the necessary blood glucose prerequisite and keep up with it consistently to encounter great wellbeing and forestall or defer complexities of diabetes.

Different method for infusing insulin include:

High-pressure air jet injector Syringe Insulin tub pump

Other measures expected to treat type 1 and 2 diabetes include Careful meal planning

Healthy eating

Healthy weight management Frequent blood sugar test Regular exercise Medications.

Glucagon for emergency management of hypoglycemia

Additional Information Regarding Nutritional Goals for Type 2 Diabetic Patients

Carbohydrates

Dietary carbs from vegetables, natural products, beans, dull food sources, cereals, bread, other grain items, vegetables, vegetables, natural products, dairy items, and added sugars ought to give the biggest part of a singular's energy necessities both the sum ate and the wellspring of starch impact blood glucose and insulin reactions. The expressions "basic" and "complex" ought not be utilized to group starches since they don't assist with deciding the effect of sugars on blood glucose levels. Keep away from natural product juices, canned natural products, or dried leafy foods new organic products all things considered. You might eat new vegetables and frozen or canned vegetables.

Protein

Protein is found in poultry, meat, fish, beans, dairy items and a few vegetables. Consume a greater amount of poultry and fish than red meat and cut back additional excess from all meat. Stay away from poultry skin. Pick nonfat or diminished fat dairies, like cheeses and yogurts. Current verification shows people with diabetes have similar protein essentials to those of everyone. Despite the fact that protein is significant for the excitement of insulin discharge, abundance utilization might add to the pathogenesis of diabetic nephropathy.

Fats

Various investigations demonstrate high-fat weight control diet can debilitate glucose obstruction and cause atherosclerotic coronary illness, dyslipidemia, and obesity.

Research in like manner shows these identical metabolic abnormalities are overseen or improved by lessening immersed fat admission. Current ideas on fat admission for everybody apply similarly to people with diabetes. Decreasing the admission of soaked fat by 10 percent or less and cholesterol admission to 300 mg/d or less. Research proposes monounsaturated fat (like nuts, fish, olive oil, canola oil, seeds, and so on) may emphatically influence greasy oils and glycemic control in specific individuals with diabetes. Sugars

Before, sugar aversion has been one of the major healthful guidance for individuals with diabetes. Nonetheless, research has shown that sugars are an indispensable piece of a sound eating regimen for diabetes, particularly sugar gotten from vegetables, natural products, and dairy items. Added sugars, for instance, sugar-improved and table sugar items, make up around 10 percent of the everyday response energy needs. Refined sucrose gives a lower blood glucose than many refined starches. Food varieties containing sugars

fluctuate in physiological impacts and dietary benefit. For instance, sucrose and pressed squeezed orange have similar blood glucose impacts however contain various supplements and minerals. Polishing off entire foods grown from the ground juices makes blood glucose focuses top somewhat prior yet fall more rapidly than drinking a practically identical carb part of white bread.

The Relationship Between Nutrients and Diabetes

People who have diabetes have abundance sugar in their blood. Thusly, overseeing diabetes implies dealing with your glucose level through the utilization of food wealthy in infusion. The supplements in prosperity. The right supplement decisions will assist you with controlling your glucose level. Eating food reach in the right supplements is one of the essential things you can do to assist with controlling diabetes. There isn't one explicit"diabetes diet" for individuals experiencing diabetes. but a dietician can work with you to design a meal plan to guide you on what sorts of food to eat and what snacks to have at eating times. A nutritious eating regimen comprises of: specific what you supplements or through insulin eat is associated your general 20 percent calories from protein

40 percent -60 percent from carbohydrates. 30 percent or lesser calories from fat

Your eating routine ought to likewise be low in salt, cholesterol, and added sugar

Contrary to conviction eating some sugar doesn't bring on some issues for the vast majority who have diabetes. Nonetheless, it's essential to watch how much sugar you eat and ensure it's important for a reasonable diet. As a general rule, every dinner ought to have the accompanying nutrients:

2-5 choices (or up to 60 grams) of carbohydrates One choice of protein A certain amount of fat

Sunrise Smoothie Bowl

Prep time: 5 minutes | Cook time: 0 minutes | Serves 1 ½ cup (63 g) frozen raspberries

½ cup (72 g) frozen strawberries

½ enormous banana

½ cup (50 g) cauliflower florets

½ cup (100 g) plain nonfat Greek yogurt Water, as needed

tbsp (5 g) unsweetened coconut drops 2 tbsp (14 g) coarsely hacked walnuts

1. In a powerful blender, consolidate the raspberries, strawberries, banana, cauliflower, and yogurt. Mix the fixings until they are smooth, adding water on a case by case basis to arrive at the ideal consistency. 2. Empty the smoothie into a bowl and top it with the coconut pieces and walnuts. Calorie: 336 | fat: 14g | protein: 17g | carbs: 44g | sugars: 21g | fiber: 12g | sodium: 69mg

Rancheros Huevos Coddled

Time to prepare: 5 minutes | Time to cook: 10 minutes Serves
2 tbsp. unsalted butter 4 massive eggs

1 cup depleted cooked dark beans, or 66 percent of a 15-ounce
can of depleted cooked dark beans, flushed and drained
12 cup thick tomato salsa, two 7-inch corn or whole wheat
tortillas, warmed (for example, Pace brand) 2 cups romaine
lettuce, shredded

1 tablespoon fresh cilantro, hacked 2 tbsp. Cotija cheese,
grated

1. Fill the Instant Pot with 1 cup water and a silicone steam
rack that has been used for a long time. (Use the wire metal
steam rack and a domestically manufactured sling if you don't
have the long-ago taken care of rack.) 2. Spread 12 teaspoon
margarine in each of four 4-ounce ramekins. In each ramekin,
crack one egg. In the saucepan, place the ramekins on the
steam rack. 3. Set the Pressure Release to Sealing and secure
the lid. Set the cooking time for 3 minutes at low tension
on the Steam setting. (It will take around 5 minutes for the
pot to warm up to straining temperature before the cooking
procedure begins.) 4. While the eggs are cooking, reheat the
beans in a small saucepan over low heat for about 5 minutes,
stirring occasionally. Remove the saucepan from the heat by
covering it. (Alternatively, microwave the beans for 1 minute
in a clean bowl.) Cover the beans and keep them warm until

ready to serve.) 5. When the cooking program is finished, let the pressure to naturally drop for 5 minutes before switching the Pressure Expel to Venting to release any leftover steam. Handle the handles of the steam rack and carefully remove it out of the pot while wearing hotness-safe gloves. 6. To serve, place a hot tortilla on each dish and ladle 12 cup of beans onto each tortilla. To loosen the egg, run a knife down the inside edge of each ramekin, then unmold two eggs onto the beans on each tortilla. Top the eggs with the salsa and lettuce, cilantro, and cheddar cheese. Serve immediately.

112 calories | 8 grams of fat | 8 grams of protein | 3 grams of carbohydrates | 0 grams of sugars | 0 grams of fiber | 297 milligrams of sodium

Farro with Berries and Walnuts for Breakfast

Time to prepare: 8 minutes | Time to cook: 10 minutes 6 people

1 cup rinsed and depleted farro 14 teaspoon fit salt 1 cup unsweetened almond milk

12 tsp vanilla extract (unadulterated) 1 tablespoon pure maple syrup 1 teaspoon cinnamon powder

12 cup blueberries, raspberries, or strawberries, freshly picked (or a blend) 6 tablespoons walnuts, cleaved

Combine the farro, almond milk, 1 cup water, salt, vanilla, cinnamon, and maple syrup in an electric tension cooker. 2. Secure the lid by closing and locking it. Set the valve to the "fix" position. 3. Cook for 10 minutes on high pressure. 4. When the cooking is finished, let the pressure naturally relax for 10 minutes before quickly releasing any leftover pressure. Press the Cancel button. 5. When the pin falls out, open the lid and remove it. 6. Toss the farro together. Spoon into dishes and top with 14 cup berries and 1 tbsp walnuts for each serving.

Serving Size

189 calories | 5 grams of fat | 5 grams of protein | 32 grams of carbohydrates | 6 grams of sugar | 3 grams of fiber | 111 milligrams of sodium

Avocado Toast Mi-So Love

Time to prepare: 5 minutes | Time to cook: 2 minutes | Servings: 4 1 cut yielded grain bread.

12 tblsp chickpea miso (or other gentle seasoned miso) 14 cup ready-to-eat avocado a squeeze of lemon juice (about 12) a teaspoon of dietary yeast a couple pinches of sea salt (discretionary) To taste, freshly ground dark pepper

a small bunch of chopped lettuce or kid spinach, or a thick sliced ripe tomato

1. Start by toasting the bread. Spread approximately 12 teaspoon of miso on each cut while it's still heated. Add a squeeze of lemon juice and a pinch of salt to the avocado and mix well. Sprinkle with pepper and nutritional yeast (if using). Cut tomatoes, lettuce, or spinach may be added on the top.

250 calories per serving | 8 grams of fat | 7 grams of protein | 38 grams of carbohydrates | 4 grams of sugars | 6 grams of fiber | 1190 milligrams of sodium

Oats with Mixed Berries

Time to prepare: 5 minutes | Time to cook: 0 minutes | Servings: 1 2 12 cup oats, rolled

1 tablespoon chia seeds, ground 4 or 5 dates that have been pitted

1/8 teaspoon nutmeg or cinnamon

14 teaspoon almond extract (discretionary) 1 cup + 2-3 tablespoons low-fat nondairy milk + a pinch of sea salt 114 cup fresh or frozen raspberries

1. Combine the oats, chia, dates, cinnamon, almond separate (if using), salt, and 1 cup of the milk in a blender. Until recently, puree was consolidated. Toss in 1 cup of raspberries and purée once more to combine. Using a spatula, transfer the mixture to a basin or container and stir in the remaining 14 cup berries. For the time being, cover and keep refrigerated

(or for a long time, if eating as a tidbit). If preferred, thin with an additional 2 to 3 tablespoons of milk before serving.

Serving Size

267 calories | 5 grams of fat | 8 grams of protein | 53 grams of carbohydrates | 20 grams of sugars | 16 grams of fiber | 199 milligrams of sodium

Omelet with Veggies

Time to prepare: 15 minutes | Time to cook: 10 minutes | Servings: 4 1 tablespoon sliced red ringer pepper 1 teaspoon olive or canola oil 1 tablespoon onion, sliced

14 cup fresh, sliced mushrooms

12 cup sans fat egg item or 2 beaten eggs 1 cup roughly filled new kid spinach leaves, washed 1 teaspoon of water

1 tsp salt 1 tsp pepper 1 tsp pepper 1 tsp pepper 1 t Cheddar is a kind of cheese.

1. Heat oil in an 8-inch nonstick skillet over medium-high heat. Toss in the chile pepper, onion, and mushrooms with the oil. Cook for 2 minutes, stirring often, until onion is soft. Add the spinach and simmer, stirring constantly, until the spinach shrivels. Transfer the veggies from the dish to the small bowl. 2 In a medium mixing bowl, whisk together the egg, water, salt, and pepper with a fork or a race until well combined. Warm the same skillet on a medium-high heat setting. Empty the egg

mixture into the container as quickly as possible. Straightaway mix while rapidly moving skillet back and forth over heat. As the eggs thicken, use a spatula to constantly spread them over the lower part of the dish. Allow to sit for a few moments over low heat to gently brown the bottom half of the omelet. Avoid overcooking; the omelet will continue to cook after collapsing. 3 Place the cooked veggie mixture on top of a part of the omelet and sprinkle with cheddar cheese. Place the second half of the omelet on top of the veggies using a spatula. Slide out of the dish onto a platter with care. Serve right away.

140 calories per serving | 5 grams of fat | 16 grams of protein | 6 grams of carbohydrates | 3 grams of sugars | 2 grams of fiber | 470 milligrams of sodium

Breakfast Bake with Rice

Time to prepare: 10 minutes | Time to cook: 20 minutes | Servings: 4

114 cup vanilla non-dairy milk, reduced in fat 1 tablespoon chia seeds, ground

212 cup cooked short-grain brown rice, cut into cups (yet not overripe) bananas (approximately 2–212 medium bananas) 1 cup apple (hacked)

a couple of teaspoons of raisins (discretionary) a pinch of cinnamon

12 tsp vanilla essence (unadulterated)

14 teaspoon nutmeg, freshly ground (discretionary) 1/8 teaspoon sea salt, rounded

almond feast (2 tablespoons) (or 1 tablespoon tigernut flour, for sans nut option) 2 tablespoons sugar de coco

1. Preheat the oven to 400 degrees Fahrenheit. 2. Combine the milk, ground chia, and 1 cup of rice in a blender or food processor. Puree until the mixture is completely smooth. Combine the mixed blend, bananas, apple, raisins (if using), cinnamon, vanilla, nutmeg (if using), salt, and the remaining 112 cup rice in a large mixing bowl. To thoroughly unite the pieces, mix them together. Place the mixture in a baking dish (8" x 8" or similar size). Combine the almond meal and sugar in a small bowl and sprinkle over the rice mixture. Bake for 15 minutes with the foil on, then remove it and bake for another 5 minutes. Remove from the oven and set aside to cool for 5 to 10 minutes before serving.

Serving Size

334 calories | 5 grams of fat | 7 grams of protein | 69 grams of carbohydrates | 22 grams of sugars | 7 grams of fiber | 145 milligrams of sodium

Sausage, potato, and egg Frittata

Time to prepare: 30 minutes | Time to cook: 20 minutes | Servings: 6 4 4 defrosted frozen soy-protein breakfast frankfurter joins (from an 8-oz box) 1 teaspoon defrosted olive oil (1 teaspoon olive oil oz. pack) 8 egg whites or 4 eggs

14 cup (fat-free) (skim) milk

a quarter teaspoon of salt

1/8 teaspoon basil leaves, dried

1/8 teaspoon oregano leaves, dried

112 cup plums, slashed (Roma) tomatoes

12 cup Asiago cheddar and mozzarella crumbles with garlic (2 oz) If desired, season with pepper. If desired, chopped green onion

1. Cut each frankfurter link into eight pieces. Heat the oil in a 10-inch nonstick skillet over medium heat. Cook for 6 to 8 minutes, stirring occasionally, until frankfurter and potatoes are golden brown. 2 In a small bowl, whisk together the eggs and milk with a fork or a rush until thoroughly combined. Pour the egg mixture over the potato mixture. Cook uncovered for 5 minutes over medium-low heat; as the mixture sets on the bottom and sides, tenderly lift cooked segments with spatula to allow flimsy, uncooked pieces to stream to the bottom. Cook until the eggs are thickened all the way through but not completely sodden; avoid constant blending. 3 Season

eggs with salt, basil, oregano, tomatoes, and cheddar cheese. Reduce the heat to low, cover, and cook for about 5 minutes, or until the focus is set and the cheddar has melted. Season with salt, pepper, and green onion. Serving Size

280 calories | 12 g fat | 17 g protein | 26 g carbs | 5 g sugar | 3 g fiber | 590 mg sodium

Sundae with Yogurt

Time to prepare: 5 minutes | Time to cook: 0 minutes | Servings: 1 a third of a cup of plain nonfat Greek yogurt

14 cup berries, blended (blueberries, strawberries, blackberries) 2 tablespoons chopped cashews, pecans, or almonds 1 tablespoon flaxseed, ground

2 shredded new mint leaves

1. Place the yogurt in a small bowl. 2. Add the berries, nuts, and flaxseed on top. 2. Garnish with mint leaves and serve.

238 calories per serving | 11 g fat | 21 g protein | 16 g carbs | 9 g sugars | 4 g fiber | 64 mg sodium

Toast topped with avocado and goat cheese

5 minutes to prepare | 10 minutes to cook | 4 servings 2 whole wheat meager cut bread, 2 slices

avocado (12 pound)

2 tbsp goat cheddar (disintegrated) to taste with salt

1. Toast the bread until it is seared in a toaster oven or grill. 2. Peel the avocado and remove the tissue. Pound the avocado tissue in a medium mixing bowl with a fork. Onto the toast, spread it. 3. Top with goat cheddar and a light seasoning of salt and pepper. 4. Serve with any additional garnishes.

137 calories per serving | 6 grams of fat | 5 grams of protein | 18 grams of carbohydrates | 0 grams of sugar | 5 grams of fiber | 195 milligrams of sodium

Granola with Cinnamon & Walnuts

10 minute prep | 30 minute cook time (16 people)

rolled oats (four cups) 1 pound chopped pecans

1 teaspoon ground cinnamon 12 cup pepitas 14 teaspoon salt 1 t. ginger powder

12 CUP COCONUT OIL, WHICH HAS BEEN REMOVED

12 cup fruit purée, unsweetened 12 CUP DRIED CHERRIES 1 TEASPOON VANILLA EXTRACT

Preheat the oven to 350 degrees Fahrenheit (180 degrees Celsius) and preheat the broiler. Use material paper to cover a baking sheet. 2. Combine the oats, pecans, pepitas, cinnamon, and ginger in a large mixing bowl. 3. Mix the coconut oil, fruit purée, and vanilla extract in a large measuring cup. Pour the wet mixture over the dry mixture and thoroughly combine. 4. Place the mixture on a baking sheet that has been prepared beforehand. Cook, stirring halfway through, for 30 minutes. Remove the granola from the heat and let it cool completely before eating. Mix in the dried cherries after breaking up the granola into pieces. 5. Store in an airtight container at room temperature for up to 2 weeks.

224 calories per serving | 15 grams fat | 5 grams protein | 20 grams carbohydrates | 5 grams sugars | 3 grams fiber

Cover and keep warm in the skillet. 7. Transfer the patties to a serving plate using an open spatula. Combine the cornstarch and water in a small mixing bowl. Select the Sauté setting after pressing the Cancel button to restart the cooking program. When the sauce has thickened to the consistency of a stew, stir in the cornstarch mixture and allow to bubble for 1 minute, or until thickened. To turn off your Instant Pot, press the Cancel button. 8. Toss the patties in the sauce and serve. With the cauliflower, serve immediately.

362 calories per serving | 21 grams of fat | 33 grams of protein | 21 grams of carbohydrates | 4 grams of sugar | 6 grams of fiber

Cherry-Sauced Pork Medallions

25 minutes to prepare | 6 to 8 minutes to cook 4 people 1 pork tenderloin (1 to 112 pound), cut into 12-inch slices

12 tsp garlic-pepper powder olive oil, 2 tbsp

a third of a cup of cherry jam

2 tbsp shallots, chopped 1 teaspoon mustard (Dijon)

balsamic vinegar, 1 tblsp 1 finely chopped garlic clove

Using the garlic-pepper mixture, season both sides of the pork. 2 1 teaspoon of oil, heated over medium-high heat in a 12-inch skillet Cook, turning once, for 6 to 8 minutes, until pork is seared and a meat thermometer inserted into the focus reads 145°F. Remove the pork and keep it warm in the skillet. 3 Blend the remaining teaspoon oil, the jam, shallots, mustard, vinegar, and garlic in the same skillet, scraping any earthy colored bits from the bottom. The temperature rises to the point where it starts to boil. Reduce heat to low; cover and simmer for 10 minutes, or until liquid has been reduced to about 12 cup. Over the pork slices, spoon the sauce.

330 calories per serving | 7 grams of fat | 23 grams of protein | 44 grams of carbohydrates | 30 grams of sugars | 1 gram of fiber

Pomodoro Pork Chops are a delicious way to prepare pork chops.

0 minutes to prepare | 30 minutes to cook | 6 servings

314 teaspoon fine ocean salt pound boneless pork midsection slashes, each around 513 ounces and 12 inch thick

12 tsp. black pepper, freshly ground 2 tbsp olive oil (extra virgin)

12 cup low-sodium chicken or vegetable broth 2 garlic cloves, chopped 12 teaspoon Italian seasoning 1 tblsp. depleted tricks 2 CUP CHINOIS

2 tbsp. fresh basil (hacked) or parsley (level leaf)

Serve with spiralized zucchini noodles, cauliflower "rice," or cooked whole grain pasta. For serving, lemon wedges

Using paper towels, pat the pork chops dry before seasoning all over with salt and pepper.

Heat 1 tablespoon of oil for 2 minutes on the Sauté setting on the Instant Pot. Cover the lower part of the pot with oil by whirling it around. Add half of the pork slashes in a single layer to the pan with utensils and cook for about 3 minutes, until the main side is delicately seared. Flip the cleaves and cook for another 3 minutes, or until the other side is softly seared. Placing the cleaves on a plate is the next step. Reheat the pork chops and the remaining 1 tablespoon oil.

Add the garlic to the pot and cook for about 1 minute, until it starts to foam but is still raw. In a large mixing bowl, combine the stock, Italian seasoning, and tricks, scraping any sautéed bits from the bottom of the pot with a wooden spoon and working quickly so that not much liquid evaporates. Move the pork slashes to the pot with the utensils in hand. On top of the slashes, spread the tomatoes out evenly. Set the Pressure Release to Sealing and secure the top. To reset the cooking program, press the Cancel button, then choose Pressure Cook or Manual and cook for 10 minutes at high pressure. (Before the cooking program begins, the pot will need to come up to pressure for about 5 minutes.) 5. When the cooking program is finished, allow the pressure to naturally release for at least 10 minutes before switching the Pressure Release to Venting to release any remaining steam. Open the pot and transfer the pork slashes to a serving dish with the help of the utensils. 6. Arrange the tomatoes on top of the pork slashes, along with a small amount of the cooking liquid. Serve with zucchini noodles and lemon wedges on the side, garnished with basil. Serving Size:

265 calories | 13 grams of fat | 31 grams of protein | 3 grams of carbohydrates | 2 grams of sugar | 1 gram of fiber

Vegetables & Easy Pot Roast

20-minute prep time | 35-minute cooking time Serves 6 pound toss cook, trim excess fat and chop into serving-size chunks 4 cubed, unpeeled medium potatoes

1 pound child carrots or 4 medium carrots, cut 2 thin-sliced celery ribs

1 dry onion soup mix envelope 3 c.

1. Along with the potatoes, carrots, and celery, place the pot broil lumps and vegetables in the Instant Pot. 2. Mix the onion soup mix with the water in a large mixing bowl and pour over the Instant Pot's contents. 3. Tighten the cover and check that the vent is in the fixed position. For 35 minutes, set the Instant Pot to Manual. When the cook time is up, let strain deliver normally. 325 calories per serving | 8 grams of fat | 35 grams of protein | 26 grams of carbohydrates | 6 grams of sugar | 4 grams of fiber

Pork and Couscous

20-minute prep time | 10-minute cook time Serves 5 114 cup couscous uncooked

medium yam, stripped, cut into julienne strips 1 pound pork tenderloin, thinly sliced 1 cup salsa with a stout flavor

12 cup water, 2 tbsp honey

14 cup cilantro, slashed

1 Prepare the couscous according to the package's directions. 2 Spray a 12-inch skillet with cooking splash while the couscous cooks. Cook for 2 to 3 minutes in a skillet over medium heat, stirring occasionally, until brown. 3 In a large mixing bowl, combine the yam, salsa, water, and honey. Reduce the heat to medium and allow it to bubble. Cook, covered, for 5–6 minutes, until the potato is tender, stirring occasionally. Add cilantro to the top. Over couscous, serve

pork blend. 320 calories per serving | 4 grams of fat | 23 grams of protein | 48 grams of carbohydrates | 11 grams of sugars | 3 grams of fiber

Chapter Three

Beef Curry that is Simple to Make

15-minute prep time | 10-minute cooking time Serves 6 tbsp olive oil (extra virgin) 1 teaspoon minced new ginger 1 small onion, thinly sliced three minced garlic cloves

2 tsp. coriander, ground cumin powder (1 teaspoon)

1 serrano pepper or jalapeo, cut longwise but not all the way through 1 tsp turmeric powder (14 tsp.)

pound grass-fed sirloin tip steak, top round steak, or top sirloin steak, cut into smaller pieces

new cilantro, chopped tablespoons

1. Heat the oil over medium-high heat in a large skillet. 2. Cook for 3 to 5 minutes, or until the onion is seared and mellowed. 30 seconds later, add the ginger and garlic and continue to mix until fragrant. 3. Mix the coriander, cumin, jalapeo, turmeric, and salt together in a small mixing bowl. In a skillet, combine

all of the flavorings and stir well for 1 minute. Using about 14 cup of water, deglaze the pan. 4. Stir in the hamburger for about 5 minutes, or until it's well-sautéed but still medium rare. The jalapeo should be removed. Garnish with cilantro before serving.

140 calories per serving | 7 grams of fat | 18 grams of protein | 3 grams of carbohydrates | 1 gram of sugar | 1 gram of fiber

Bunless Sloppy Joes

Prep time: 15 minutes | Cook time: 40 minutes | Serves 6 6 little sweet potatoes

1 pound (454 g) lean ground hamburger 1 onion, finely chopped carrot, finely chopped ¼ cup finely hacked mushrooms

¼ cup finely cleaved red ringer pepper 3 garlic cloves, minced teaspoons Worcestershire sauce 1 tablespoon white wine vinegar

1 (15-ounce/425-g) can low-sodium pureed tomatoes 2 tablespoons tomato paste

1. Preheat the stove to 400°F (205°C). 2. Place the yams in a solitary layer in a baking dish. Heat for 25 to 40 minutes, contingent upon the size, until they are delicate and cooked through. 3. While the yams are heating up, in an enormous skillet, cook the hamburger over medium hotness until it's

seared, splitting it up into little pieces as you mix. 4. Add the onion, carrot, mushrooms, ringer pepper, and garlic, and sauté momentarily for 1 minute. 5. Mix in the Worcestershire sauce, vinegar, pureed tomatoes, and tomato glue. Bring to a stew, lessen the hotness, and cook for 5 minutes for the flavors to merge. 6. Scoop ½ cup of the meat blend on top of each prepared potato and serve.

Per Serving calories: 372 | fat: 19g | protein: 16g | carbs: 34g | sugars: 13g | fiber: 6g | sodium: 161mg

Beef Curry

15 minutes to prepare | 10 minutes to cook | 4 servings 6 tbsp olive oil (extra virgin) 1 teaspoon minced new ginger 1 small onion, thinly sliced three minced garlic cloves

2 tsp. coriander, ground cumin powder (1 teaspoon)

1 jalapeño or serrano pepper, cut the long way yet not as far as possible through

¼ teaspoon ground turmeric ¼ teaspoon salt pound (454 g) grass-took care of sirloin tip steak, top round steak, or top sirloin steak, cut into scaled down pieces

tablespoons cleaved new cilantro

1. In an enormous skillet, heat the oil over medium high. 2. Cook for 3 to 5 minutes, or until the onion is seared and mellowed. Add the ginger and garlic, mixing consistently until

fragrant, around 30 seconds. 3. Mix the coriander, cumin, jalapeo, turmeric, and salt together in a small mixing bowl. Add the flavor combination to the skillet and mix 4. consistently for 1 moment. Using about 14 cup of water, deglaze the pan. 5. Add the hamburger and mix constantly for around 5 minutes until very much sautéed yet still medium uncommon. The jalapeo should be removed. Garnish with cilantro before serving.

Per Serving calories: 140 | fat: 7g | protein: 18g | carbs: 3g | sugars: 1g | fiber: 1g | sodium: 141mg

Asian Grilled Beef Salad

Prep time: 15 minutes | Cook time: 15 minutes | Serves 4
Dressing:

¼ cup newly pressed lime juice

1 tablespoon low-sodium tamari or sans gluten soy sauce 1 tablespoon extra-virgin olive oil 1 garlic clove, minced

1 teaspoon honey

¼ teaspoon red pepper flakes

Salad:

1 pound (454 g) grass-took care of flank steak

salt (1/4 teaspoon)

Pinch newly ground dark pepper 6 cups hacked leaf lettuce

1 cucumber, split longwise and daintily cut into half moons ½ little red onion, cut 1 carrot, cut into ribbons

¼ cup cleaved new cilantro

Make the Dressing 1. In a little bowl, whisk together the lime juice, tamari, olive oil, garlic, honey, and red pepper pieces. Set aside.

Make the Salad

1. Season the hamburger on the two sides with the salt and pepper. 2. Heat a skillet over high hotness until hot. Cook the hamburger for 3 to 6 minutes for every side, contingent upon favored doneness. Put away, rose with aluminum foil, for 10 minutes. 3. In a huge bowl, throw the lettuce, cucumber, onion, carrot, and cilantro. 4. Cut the meat meagerly contrary to what would be expected and move to the serving of mixed greens bowl. 5. Shower with the dressing and throw. Serve.

Per Serving calories: 231 | fat: 10g | protein: 26g | carbs: 10g | sugars: 4g | fiber: 2g | sodium: 349mg

Mustard Glazed Pork Chops

Prep time: 5 minutes | Cook time: 25 minutes | Serves 4 ¼ cup Dijon mustard

1 tablespoon unadulterated maple syrup 2 tablespoons rice vinegar

4 bone-in, dainty cut pork chops

1. Preheat the broiler to 400°F (205°C). 2. In a little pot, join the mustard, maple syrup, and rice vinegar. Mix to blend and bring to a stew over medium hotness. Cook for around 2 minutes until just marginally thickened. 3. In a baking dish, place the pork slashes and spoon the sauce over them, turning to cover. 4. Heat, uncovered, for 18 to 22 minutes until the juices run clear.

Per Serving calories: 257 | fat: 7g | protein: 39g | carbs: 7g | sugars: 4g | fiber: 0g | sodium: 466mg

Pork Chops with a Parmesan Crusade

Time to prepare: 10 minutes | Time to cook: 25 minutes Serves 4 cooking spray (nonstick)

4 bone-in, thinly sliced pork hacks 2 tablespoons unsalted butter

12 cup grated Parmesan cheese 3 chopped garlic cloves 14 teaspoon salt 14 teaspoon dried thyme

To taste, freshly ground dark pepper

1. Preheat the oven to 400 degrees Fahrenheit (205 degrees Celsius). Prepare a baking sheet by lining it with parchment paper and spraying it with nonstick cooking spray. 2. Arrange the pork chops on the prepared baking sheet in such a way that they do not overlap. 3. Combine the spread, cheddar, garlic, salt, thyme, and pepper in a small bowl. 2 tablespoons

cheddar mixture, pressed onto the highest point of each pork hack 4. Cook for 18 to 22 minutes, or until the pork is fully cooked and the juices run clear. Preheat the broiler to high and brown the tops for 1 to 2 minutes.

332 calories per serving | 16 g fat | 44 g protein | 1 g carbohydrates | 0 g sugars | 0 g fiber | 440 mg sodium

Roasted Pork Tenderloin with Mango Glaze

10 minutes to prepare | 20 minutes to cook | 4 servings one pound (454 g) Pork tenderloin, boneless, with superfluous fat removed 1 teaspoon rosemary, chopped

1 teaspoon freshly hacked thyme

14 teaspoon freshly ground dark pepper, separated 14 teaspoon salt, split 1 tblsp extra-virgin olive oil 1 tblsp honey 2 tblsp white wine vinegar 2 teaspoons dry cooking wine 1 tablespoon fresh ginger, minced 1 cup mango, diced

1. Preheat the oven to 400 degrees Fahrenheit (205 degrees Celsius). 2. Season the tenderloin with the rosemary, thyme, and 1/8 teaspoon salt and pepper. 3. In a broiler-safe skillet, heat the olive oil over medium-high heat and brown the tenderloin on both sides, about 5 minutes total. 4. Place the skillet under the broiler for 12 to 15 minutes, or until the pork is cooked through, the juices run clear, and the interior temperature reaches 145 degrees Fahrenheit (63 degrees Celsius). Set aside for 5 minutes on a slicing board to cool.

4. Combine the honey, vinegar, cooking wine, and ginger in a small bowl. Pour the honey mixture into a similar skillet and cook for 1 minute. Toss in the mango and cover with a towel. Purée in a blender until completely smooth. Season to taste with the remaining 1/8 teaspoon salt and 1/8 teaspoon pepper. 5. Slice the pork into rounds and serve with the mango sauce on the side.

182 calories per serving | 4 g fat | 24 g protein | 12 g carbohydrates | 10 g sugars | 1 g fiber | 240 mg sodium

Skewers of Curried Pork and Vegetables

15-minute prep time | 15-minute cook time | Serves 4 14 cup nonfat plain Greek yogurt curry powder (two tablespoons)

1 teaspoon powdered garlic

1 teaspoon turmeric powder 1 lime, zest and juice 14 teaspoon salt

1 tsp. freshly ground dark pepper

Boneless pork tenderloin, 1 pound (454 g), sliced into smaller pieces 1 cultivated red ringer pepper, sliced into 2-inch squares 1 cultivated green bell pepper, sliced into 2-inch squares 1 red onion, cut into quarters and segments

1. Combine the yogurt, curry powder, garlic powder, turmeric, lime zing, lime squeeze, salt, and pepper in a large mixing bowl. 2. Toss in the pork tenderloin chunks and stir to

combine. Refrigerate for at least 1 hour and up to 6 hours before serving. 3. Preheat the grill or the oven to medium. 4. Skewer the pork, chile peppers, and onions together on skewers.

Cook for 12 to 15 minutes on the grill or sear, flipping every 3 or 4 minutes until the pork is cooked through. Serve.

175 calories per serving | 3 grams of fat | 27 grams of protein | 10 grams of carbohydrates | 4 grams of sugars | 3 grams of fiber | 188 milligrams of sodium

Burgers made with lamb, mushrooms, and cheese

15-minute prep time | 15-minute cook time | Serves 8 ounces 4 (227 g) grass-looked after lamb in the ground

14 teaspoon salt 14 teaspoon freshly ground black pepper 8 ounces (227 g) earthy colored mushrooms, coarsely sliced

14 cup crumbled goat cheese 1 tablespoon fresh basil, minced

1. Combine the sheep, mushrooms, salt, and pepper in a large mixing bowl and blend well. 2. Combine the goat cheddar and basil in a small mixing bowl.

3. Form the sheep mixture into four patties, reserving approximately 12 cup of the mixture in the mixing dish. Make a hole in the centre of each burger and fill it with 1 tablespoon of the goat cheddar mixture. Close the burgers with the held meat mixture. To keep the meat together, firmly press it.

5. Heat the grill or an enormous skillet over medium-high hotness. Cook for 5 to 7 minutes on each side, until the burgers are cooked through. Serve.

173 calories per serving | 13 grams of fat | 11 grams of protein | 3 grams of carbohydrates | 1 gram of sugar | 0 grams of fiber | 154 milligrams of sodium

Tofu from the Southwest

Time to prepare: 10 minutes | Time to cook: 20 minutes Serves 4 312 tbsp lime juice, freshly crushed 2 tblsp maple syrup, pure and unadulterated 112 tablespoons cumin powder

1 teaspoon oregano leaves, dried 1 teaspoon stew powder

12 tbsp. paprika

12 teaspoon salt from the sea

a quarter teaspoon of allspice

1 pound (12 ounces) extra-firm tofu, cut into 14- to 12-inch thick squares and tapped to remove excess moisture

1. Combine the lime juice, syrup, cumin, oregano, stew powder, paprika, salt, and allspice in a 9" x 12" baking dish. Add the tofu and spread it out to coat both sides. Cook, flipping once, for 20 minutes, or until the marinade is retained.

Serving Size:

78 calories | 4 g fat | 7 g protein | 6 g carbohydrates | 3 g sugars | 1 g fiber | 324 mg sodium

Dal Makhani (vegan)

Time to prepare: 0 minutes | Time to cook: 55 minutes | Servings: 4 6 1 cup kidney beans, dried

13 cup urad dal, Puy lentils, or beluga lentils four cups of water

1 teaspoon sea salt (fine)

1 tablespoon avocado oil (cold-pressed) cumin seeds (1 tablespoon)

1 inch of fresh ginger, peeled and minced 4 garlic cloves, minced large yellow onion, diced cultivated and diced jalapeo chiles 1 cultivated and diced green chime pepper 1 tblsp garam masala 1 tblsp turmeric powder

cayenne pepper (1/4 teaspoon) (optional)

15-ounce can of chopped tomatoes that have been fire-simmered and liquid 2 tblsp. thick vegetarian spread tablespoons hacked new cilantro, cooked cauliflower "rice" for serving 6 tbsp coconut yogurt (plain)

1. Mix the kidney beans, urad dal, water, and salt in a medium bowl to break up the salt. Allow 12 hours for dousing. 2. Heat the oil and cumin seeds in the Instant Pot on the Sauté setting for 3 minutes, or until the seeds are bubbling, lightly toasted, and sweet-smelling. Add the ginger and garlic and cook for 1

minute, or until fragrant and gurgling. Sauté for 5 minutes, until the onion begins to soften, adding the onion, jalapeos, and ringer pepper as needed. 3. Blend in the garam masala, turmeric, cayenne (if using), and the soaked beans and their liquid. On top, pour the tomatoes and their liquid. Do not combine them. Set the Pressure Release to Sealing and secure the top. To reset the cooking program, hit the Cancel button, then choose Pressure Cook or Manual and set the cooking duration for 30 minutes at high pressure. (It will take around 15 minutes for the pot to reach up to straining temperature before the cooking procedure begins.) 5. When the cooking program is finished, wait 30 minutes for the pressure to naturally drop, then switch the Pressure Remove to Venting to release any leftover steam. Stir to incorporate the ingredients in the saucepan, then add the buttery spread. If you want a smoother texture, pour 112 cups of the dal into a blender and puree for 30 seconds, then incorporate the blended mixture into the remaining dal in the saucepan. 6. Scoop the dal on top of the cauliflower "rice" in bowls. Serve with a sprinkling of cilantro and a dollop of coconut yogurt on top.

Serving Size:

245 calories | 7 grams of fat | 11 grams of protein | 37 grams of carbohydrates | 4 grams of sugars | 10 grams of fiber | 518 milligrams of sodium

Salad de Spinach avec oeufs, tempeh bacon, et strawberries

Time to prepare: 10 minutes | Time to cook: 15 minutes Serves 4

2 tbsp soy sauce, tamari, or coconut aminos (optional) 1 tablespoon vinegar made from apple juice

1 tablespoon maple syrup, pure and unadulterated

12 teaspoon paprika (smoked) dark pepper, freshly ground

1 8-ounce tempeh bundle, cut into 18-inch thick slices 8 colossal eggs 3 tbsp extra-virgin extra-virgin olive oil

1 minced shallot\stablespoon red wine vinegar balsamic vinegar, 1 tblsp 1 teaspoon Dijon mustard\s¼ teaspoon fine ocean salt

One 6-ounce sack child spinach\shearts romaine lettuce, attacked reduced down pieces 12 new strawberries, sliced

1. In a 1-quart ziplock plastic sack, consolidate the soy sauce, juice vinegar, maple syrup, paprika, and ½ teaspoon pepper and cautiously disturb the pack to blend the fixings to make a marinade. Add the tempeh, seal the sack, and turn the pack to and fro a few times to cover the tempeh equally with the marinade. Marinate in the cooler for no less than 2 hours or as long as 24 hours. 2. Empty 1 cup water into the Instant Pot and spot the wire metal steam rack, an egg rack, or a liner crate into the pot. Delicately place the eggs on top of the rack or in the container, taking consideration not to break them. 3.

Secure the top and set the Pressure Release to Sealing. Select the Steam setting and set the cooking time for 3 minutes at high strain. (Before the cooking program begins, the pot will need to come up to strain for about 5 minutes.) 4. While the eggs\sare cooking, set up an ice shower. 5. At the point when the cooking program closes, play out a fast tension delivery by moving the Pressure Release to Venting. Open the pot and, utilizing utensils, move the eggs to the ice shower to cool. 6. Eliminate the tempeh from the marinade and blotch dry between layers of paper towels.

Discard the marinade. In an enormous nonstick skillet over medium-high hotness, warm 1 tablespoon of the oil for 2 minutes. Add the tempeh in a solitary layer and fry, turning once, for 2 to 3 minutes for every side, until well browned.

Transfer the tempeh to a plate and put away. 7. Clear out the skillet and set it over medium hotness. Add the excess 2 tablespoons oil and the shallot and sauté for around 2 minutes, until the shallot is brilliant brown. Switch off the hotness and mix in the red wine vinegar, balsamic vinegar, mustard, salt, and ¼ teaspoon pepper to make a vinaigrette. 8. In a huge bowl, consolidate the spinach and romaine. Pour in the vinaigrette and throw until every one of the leaves are delicately covered. Partition the dressed greens uniformly among four huge serving plates or shallow dishes and orchestrate the strawberries and seared tempeh on top.

Strip the eggs, cut them down the middle the long way, and spot them on top of the servings of mixed greens. Top a few toils of pepper and serve right away. Serving Size:

Calorie: 435 | fat: 25g | protein: 29g | carbs: 25g | sugars: 10g | fiber: 5g | sodium: 332mg

Chapter Four

Chile Relleno Casserole with Salsa Salad

Prep time: 10 minutes | Cook time: 55 minutes | Serves 4\sCasserole

½ cup without gluten flour, (for example, King Arthur or Cup4Cup brand) (for example, King Arthur or Cup4Cup brand) 1 teaspoon baking powder

6 huge eggs

½ cup nondairy milk or entire milk

Three 4-ounce jars fire-broiled diced green chiles, depleted 1 cup nondairy cheddar shreds or destroyed mozzarella cheddar Salad

1 head green leaf lettuce, destroyed 2 Roma tomatoes, cultivated and diced

1 cultivated and diced green chile pepper

½ little yellow onion, diced

1 jalapeño chile, cultivated and diced (discretionary) (discretionary) 2 tablespoons cleaved new cilantro

4 teaspoons extra-virgin olive oil 4 teaspoons new lime juice

⅛ teaspoon fine ocean salt

1. To make the meal: Pour 1 cup water into the Instant Pot. Spread a 7-cup round heatproof glass dish or coat with nonstick cooking shower and spot the dish on a since a long time ago took care of silicone steam rack. (On the off chance that you don't have the since quite a while ago dealt with rack, utilize the wire metal steam rack and a natively constructed sling) 2. In a medium bowl, whisk together the flour and baking powder. Add the eggs and milk and race until all around mixed, framing a hitter. Mix in the chiles and ¾ cup of the cheddar. 3. Empty the player into the pre-arranged dish and cover firmly with aluminum foil. Holding the handles of the steam rack, bring down the dish into the Instant Pot. 4. Secure the cover and set the Pressure Release to Sealing. Select the Pressure Cook or Manual setting and set the cooking time for 40 minutes at high strain. (The pot will require around 10 minutes to come up to\sstrain before the cooking program starts.) 5. When the cooking program is finished, allow the pressure to naturally release for at least 10 minutes before switching the Pressure Release to Venting to release any remaining steam. Open the pot and, wearing hotness safe

gloves, handle the handles of the steam rack and lift it out of the pot. Uncover the dish, taking consideration not to get scorched by the steam or to trickle buildup onto the meal. While the dish is as yet steaming hot, sprinkle the leftover ¼ cup cheddar uniformly on top. Allow the cheddar to soften for 5 minutes. 6. To make the serving of mixed greens: While the cheddar is dissolving, in an enormous bowl, consolidate the lettuce, tomatoes, ringer pepper, onion, jalapeño (if utilizing), cilantro, oil, lime squeeze, and salt. Throw until equally joined. 7. Cut the dish into wedges. Serve warm, with the plate of mixed greens on the side. Serving Size:

Calorie: 361 | fat: 22g | protein: 21g | carbs: 23g | sugars: 8g | fiber: 3g | sodium: 421mg

Green Goddess White Bean Dip

Prep time: 1 minutes | Cook time: 45 minutes | Makes 3 cups 1 cup dried naval force, extraordinary Northern, or\scannellini beans water (four cups) 2 teaspoons fine ocean salt\s3 tablespoons new lemon juice

¼ cup extra-virgin olive oil, in addition to 1 tablespoon\s¼ cup solidly pressed new level leaf parsley leaves 1 bundle chives, chopped

Leaves from 2 tarragon branches black pepper, freshly ground

1. Consolidate the beans, water, and 1 teaspoon of the salt in the Instant Pot and mix to break down the salt. 2. Secure the cover and set the Pressure Release to Sealing. Select the Bean/Chili, Pressure Cook, or Manual setting and set the cooking time for 30 minutes at high tension on the off chance that utilizing naval force or Great Northern beans or 40 minutes at high strain if utilizing cannellini beans. (Before the cooking program begins, the pot will need about 15 minutes to come up to strain.) 3. When the cooking program ends, let the pressure release naturally for 15 minutes, then move the Pressure Release to Venting to release any remaining steam. Open the pot and scoop out and save ½ cup of the cooking fluid. Wearing hotness safe gloves, lift out the internal pot and channel the beans in a colander. 4. In a food processor or blender, consolidate the beans,\s½ cup cooking fluid, lemon juice, ¼ cup olive oil, ½ teaspoon parsley, chives, tarragon, staying 1 teaspoon salt, and ½ teaspoon pepper. Cycle or mix on medium speed, halting to scratch down the sides of the compartment on a case by case basis, for around 1 moment, until the blend is smooth. 5. Move the plunge to a serving bowl. Shower with the leftover 1 tablespoon olive oil and sprinkle with a couple of toils of pepper. The dunk will keep in a sealed shut compartment in the fridge for as long as multi week. Serve at room temperature or chilled.

Calorie: 70 | fat: 5g | protein: 3g | carbs: 8g | sugars: 1g | fiber: 4g | sodium: 782mg

Vietnamese Meatball Lollipops with Dipping Sauce

Prep time: 30 minutes | Cook time: 20 minutes | Serves 12

Meatballs

1¼ lb lean (essentially 90 percent) ground turkey

¼ cup cleaved water chestnuts (from 8-oz can), drained ¼ cup slashed new cilantro 1 tablespoon cornstarch tablespoons fish sauce

½ teaspoon pepper cloves garlic, finely hacked Dipping Sauce

¼ cup water

¼ cup decreased sodium soy sauce 2 tablespoons stuffed brown sugar

2 tablespoons slashed new chives or green onions 2 tablespoons lime juice

2 cloves garlic, finely chopped

½ teaspoon squashed red pepper About 24 (6-inch) bamboo skewers

1 Heat broiler to 400°F. Line treat sheet with foil; splash with cooking shower (or utilize nonstick foil). 2 In huge bowl, consolidate all meatball fixings until very much blended. Shape into 1¼-inch meatballs. On treat sheet, place meatballs 1 inch separated. Heat 20 minutes, turning partially through baking, until thermometer embedded in focal point of

meatballs peruses essentially 165°F. 3 Meanwhile, in 1-quart pan, heat all plunging sauce fixings over low hotness until sugar is broken down; put away. 4 Insert bamboo sticks into cooked meatballs; place on serving plate. Present with warm plunging sauce.

Serving Size:

Calorie: 80 | fat: 2.5g | protein: 10g | carbs: 5g | sugars: 3g | fiber: 0g | sodium: 440mg

Calorie: 307 | fat: 20g | protein: 6g | carbs: 33g | sugars: 13g | fiber: 13g | sodium: 173mg

Baked Berry Cups with Crispy Cinnamon Wedges

Prep time: 25 minutes | Cook time: 30 minutes | Serves 4 teaspoons sugar ¾ teaspoon ground cinnamon Butter-flavor cooking spray adjusted carb entire wheat tortilla (6 inch)

¼ cup sugar tablespoons white entire wheat flour 1 teaspoon ground orange strip, whenever wanted 1½ cups new blueberries

1½ cups new raspberries

About 1 cup without fat whipped cream beating (from spray can)

Heat stove to 375°F. In sandwich-size resealable food-stockpiling plastic pack, consolidate 2 teaspoons sugar and ½ teaspoon of the cinnamon. Utilizing cooking shower, splash the two sides of tortilla, around 3 seconds for each side; cut tortilla into 8 wedges. In sack with cinnamon- sugar, add wedges; seal pack. Shake to cover wedges equally. 2 On ungreased treat sheet, spread out wedges. Prepare 7 to 9 minutes, turning once, until simply starting to fresh (wedges will keep on crisping while at the same time cooling). Cool around 15 minutes. 3 Meanwhile, splash 4 (6- oz) custard cups or ramekins with cooking shower; place cups on another treat sheet. In little bowl, mix ¼ cup sugar, the flour, orange strip and remaining ¼ teaspoon cinnamon until mixed. In medium bowl, tenderly throw berries with sugar combination; partition equally among custard cups. 4 Bake 15 minutes; mix tenderly. Prepare 5 to 7 minutes longer or until fluid is rising around edges. Cool no less than 15 minutes. 5 To serve, top each cup with about ¼ cup whipped cream besting; serve tortilla wedges with berry cups. Serve warm. Serving Size:

Calorie: 180 | fat: 2g | protein: 3g | carbs: 37g | sugars: 25g | fiber: 7g | sodium: 60mg

Berry Smoothie Pops

5 minutes to prepare | 0 minutes to cook | 4 servings 6 cups frozen blended berries

½ cup unsweetened plain almond milk 1 cup plain nonfat Greek yogurt

2 tablespoons hemp seeds

1. Place every one of the fixings in a blender and cycle until finely mixed. 2. Fill 6 clean ice pop shape and addition sticks. 3. Freeze for 3 to 4 hours until firm.

Serving Size:

Calorie: 70 | fat: 2g | protein: 5g | carbs: 9g | sugars: 2g | fiber: 3g | sodium: 28mg

Instant Pot Tapioca Prep time: 10 minutes | Cook time: 7 minutes | Serves 6

2 cups water

1 cup little pearl tapioca ½ cup sugar 4 eggs

½ cup vanished skim milk

Sugar substitute to approach ¼ cup sugar 1 teaspoon vanilla

Fruit of decision, optional

1. Join water and custard in Instant Pot. 2. Secure top and ensure vent is set to fixing. Press Manual and set for 5 minutes. 3. Play out a fast delivery. Press Cancel, eliminate top, and press Sauté. 4. Whisk together eggs and vanished milk. Gradually add to the Instant Pot, blending continually so the eggs don't scramble. 5. Stir in the sugar substitute until it's dissolved, press Cancel, then stir in the vanilla. 6. Allow to cool thoroughly, then refrigerate at least 4 hours. Serving Size:

Calorie: 262 | fat: 3g | protein: 6g | carbs: 50g | sugars: 28g | fiber: 0g | sodium: 75mg

Oatmeal Cookies

Prep time: 5 minutes | Cook time: 15 minutes | Serves 16 ¾ cup almond flour

¾ cup antiquated oats

¼ cup destroyed unsweetened coconut 1 teaspoon baking powder

1 teaspoon ground cinnamon

¼ teaspoon salt ¼ cup unsweetened fruit purée 1 huge egg tablespoon unadulterated maple syrup 2 tablespoons coconut oil, melted

1. Preheat the stove to 350°F. 2. In a medium blending bowl, consolidate the almond flour, oats, coconut, baking powder, cinnamon, and salt, and blend well. 3. In another medium bowl, consolidate the fruit purée, egg, maple syrup, and coconut oil, and blend. Mix the wet blend into the dry combination. 4. Structure the batter into balls somewhat greater than a tablespoon and spot on a baking sheet, leaving somewhere around 1 inch between them. Prepare for 12 minutes until the treats are recently sautéed. Eliminate from the stove and let cool for 5 minutes.

5. Utilizing a spatula, eliminate the treats and cool on a rack.

Serving Size:

Calorie: 76 | fat: 6g | protein: 2g | carbs: 5g | sugars: 1g | fiber: 1g | sodium: 57mg

Raspberry Nice Cream

Prep time: 5 minutes | Cook time: 0 minutes | Serves 3 cups frozen, cut, overripe bananas 2 cups frozen or new raspberries Pinch of ocean salt

1-2 tablespoons coconut nectar or 1-1½ tablespoons unadulterated maple syrup

1. In a food processor or high velocity blender, consolidate the bananas, raspberries, salt, and 1 tablespoon of the nectar or syrup. Puree until smooth. Taste, and add the leftover nectar or syrup, whenever wanted. Serve promptly, on the off chance that you like a delicate serve consistency, or move to a water/air proof holder and freeze for an hour or more, assuming you like a firmer texture.

Serving Size:

Calorie: 193| fat: 1g | protein: 3g | carbs: 47g | sugars: 24g | fiber: 13g | sodium: 101mg

Chocolate Baked Bananas

Prep time: 10 minutes | Cook time: 8 to 10 minutes | Serves 5 4-5 enormous ready bananas, cut lengthwise 2 tablespoons coconut nectar or unadulterated maple syrup 1 tablespoon cocoa powder Couple squeezes ocean salt

2 tablespoons nondairy chocolate chips (for finishing)

tablespoon slashed walnuts, pecans, almonds, or pumpkin seeds (for finishing)

1. Line a baking sheet with material paper and preheat broiler to 450°F. Place bananas on the material. In a bowl, blend the coconut nectar or maple syrup with the cocoa powder and salt. Mix well to completely join. Sprinkle the chocolate combination over the bananas. Heat for 8 to 10 minutes, until bananas are relaxed and caramelized. Sprinkle on chocolate chips and nuts, and serve.

Per Serving Calorie: 146 | fat: 3g | protein: 2g | carbs: 34g | sugars: 18g | fiber: 4g | sodium: 119mg

Greek Yogurt Berry Smoothie Pops

Prep time: 5 minutes | Cook time: 0 minutes | Serves 6 cups frozen blended berries

½ cup unsweetened plain almond milk 1 cup plain nonfat Greek yogurt

2 tablespoons hemp seeds

1. Place every one of the fixings in a blender and interaction until finely blended.

Pour into 6 clean ice pop shape and supplement sticks. 2. Freeze for 3 to 4 hours until firm.

Per Serving calories: 70 | fat: 2g | protein: 5g | carbs: 9g | sugars: 2g | fiber: 3g | sodium: 28mg

Grilled Peach and Coconut Yogurt Bowls

5 minutes to prepare | 10 minutes to cook | 4 servings 4

2 peaches, divided and pitted

½ cup plain nonfat Greek yogurt 1 teaspoon unadulterated vanilla extract

¼ cup unsweetened dried coconut flakes

2 tablespoons unsalted pistachios, shelled and broken into pieces

1. Preheat the oven to high. Orchestrate the rack in the nearest position to the broiler.

In a shallow container, organize the peach parts, cut-side up. Cook for 6 to 8 minutes until seared, delicate, and hot. 2. In a little bowl, blend the yogurt and vanilla.

Spoon the yogurt into the depression of each peach half. 3. Sprinkle 1 tablespoon of coconut drops and 1½ teaspoons of pistachios over each peach half. Serve warm.

Per Serving calories: 102 | fat: 5g | protein: 5g | carbs: 11g | sugars: 8g | fiber: 2g | sodium: 12mg

Frozen Chocolate Peanut Butter Bites

Prep time: 5 minutes | Cook time: 0 minutes | Serves 32

1 cup coconut oil, melted ¼ cup cocoa powder

¼ cup honey ¼ cup normal nut butter

1. Pour the softened coconut oil into a medium bowl. Rush in the cocoa powder, honey, and peanut butter. 2. Move the blend to ice block plate in segments around 1½ teaspoons each. 3. Freeze for 2 hours or until prepared to serve.

Per Serving calories: 80 | fat: 8g | protein: 1g | carbs: 3g | sugars: 2g | fiber: 0g | sodium: 20mg

Dark Chocolate Almond Butter Cups

Prep time: 15 minutes | Cook time: 0 minutes | Serves 12
½ cup regular almond butter 1 tbsp maple syrup, pure and unadulterated 1 cup dim chocolate chips

1 tablespoon coconut oil

1. Line a 12-cup biscuit tin with cupcake liners. 2. In a medium bowl, blend the almond spread and maple syrup. In the event that essential, heat in the microwave to mellow marginally. 3. Spoon around 2 teaspoons of the almond spread blend into every biscuit cup and press down to fill. 4. In a twofold kettle or the microwave, dissolve the chocolate chips. Mix in the coconut oil, and blend well to consolidate. 5. Drop 1 tablespoon of chocolate on top of every almond margarine

cup. 6. Freeze for something like 30 minutes to set. Defrost for 10 minutes before serving.

Per Serving calories: 101 | fat: 8g | protein: 3g | carbs: 6g | sugars: 4g | fiber: 1g | sodium: 32mg

No-Bake Carrot Cake Bites

Prep time: 15 minutes | Cook time: 0 minutes | Serves 20 ½ cup antiquated oats 2 medium carrots, slashed 6 dates, pitted ½ cup cleaved walnuts

½ cup coconut flour

2 tablespoons hemp seeds 2 tblsp maple syrup (unprocessed) 1 teaspoon ground cinnamon

½ teaspoon ground nutmeg

1. In a blender container, consolidate the oats and carrots, and cycle until finely ground. Move to a bowl. 2. Add the dates and pecans to the blender and interaction until coarsely hacked. Return the oat-carrot combination to the blender and add the coconut flour, hemp seeds, maple syrup, cinnamon, and nutmeg. Process until very much blended. 3. Utilizing your hands, shape the batter into balls about the size of a tablespoon. 4. Store in the fridge in a water/air proof holder for up to 1 week.

Per Serving calories: 68 | fat: 3g | protein: 2g | carbs: 10g | sugars: 6g | fiber: 2g | sodium: 6mg

Creamy Strawberry Crepes

Prep time: 10 minutes | Cook time: 10 minutes | Serves 4 ½ cup antiquated oats

1 cup unsweetened plain almond milk 1 egg

3 teaspoons honey, partitioned Nonstick cooking spray

2 ounces (57 g) low-fat cream cheese

¼ cup low-fat curds 2 cups cut strawberries

1. In a blender container, process the oats until they take after flour. Add the almond milk, egg, and 1½ teaspoons honey, and interaction until smooth. 2. Heat an enormous skillet over medium hotness. Shower with nonstick cooking splash to cover. 3. Add ¼ cup of oat player to the container and straightaway whirl around to cover the lower part of the skillet and let cook for 2 to 3 minutes. At the point when the edges start to become brown, flip the crepe with a spatula and cook until gently carmelized and firm, around 1 moment. Move to a plate. Proceed with the leftover player, splashing the skillet with nonstick cooking shower prior to adding more hitter. Put the cooked crepes away, inexactly covered with aluminum foil, while you make the filling. 4. Clean the blender jar, then combine the cream cheese, cottage cheese, and remaining 1½ teaspoons honey, and process until smooth. 5. Fill each crepe with 2 tablespoons of the cream cheddar combination, finished off with ¼ cup of strawberries. Serve.

149 calories per serving | 6 g fat | 6 g protein | 20 g carbohydrates | 10 g sugars | 3 g fiber

Brownies with a Swirl of Cream Cheese

Time to prepare: 10 minutes | Time to cook: 20 minutes | Number of servings: 4 12\seggs

14 cup applesauce (non-sweetened)

14 cup unsweetened cocoa powder 14 cup coconut oil, heated tablespoons pure maple syrup, divided

a quarter cup of coconut flour, a quarter teaspoon of salt, and a quarter teaspoon of baking powder

a tbsp. cream cheese (low-fat)

Preheat the oven to 350 degrees Fahrenheit (180 degrees Celsius) and preheat the broiler. An 8-by-8-inch baking dish should be lightly greased. 2. Whisk the eggs, fruit purée, coconut oil, and 2 tablespoons maple syrup together in a large mixing bowl.

3. Blend in the cocoa powder and coconut flour until thoroughly combined. Sprinkle the salt and baking powder evenly over the top and mix thoroughly to combine. Transfer the mixture to a baking dish that has already been prepared. 4. Microwave the cream cheddar for 10 to 20 seconds in a small microwave-safe bowl until softened. Blend in the remaining 1 tablespoon of maple syrup. 5. Using a toothpick or chopstick,

whirl the cream cheddar onto the player on a superficial level. Heat for 20 minutes, or until the truth is revealed by a toothpick inserted in the center. Cut into 12 squares once cool. 6. Refrigerate for up to 5 days in a covered container.

84 calories per serving | 6 g fat | 2 g protein | 6 g carbohydrates | 4 g sugars | 2 g fiber

Cookies made with maple syrup and oats.

5 minutes to prepare | 15 minutes to cook | 6 servings 14 cup crushed unsweetened coconut 16 34 cup almond flour 34 cup antiquated oats 1 tbsp flour 1tsp cinnamon powder

14 cup unsweetened fruit purée 14 teaspoon salt one enormous egg

1 tbsp maple syrup, pure and unadulterated 2 tbsp. melted coconut oil

Preheat the oven to 350 degrees Fahrenheit (180 degrees Celsius) and preheat the broiler. 2. Combine the almond flour, oats, coconut, baking powder, cinnamon, and salt in a medium mixing bowl and well combine. 3. Blend the fruit purée, egg, maple syrup, and coconut oil together in a separate medium bowl. Blend the wet and dry ingredients together. 4. Form the mixture into balls about the size of a tablespoon and place on a baking sheet, spacing them about an inch apart. Heat for 12 minutes, or until the treats are hot off the grill. Allow 5 minutes to cool after removing from the broiler. 5. Remove the goodies with a spatula and set aside to cool.

76 calories per serving | 6 grams of fat | 2 grams of protein | 5 grams of carbohydrates | 1 gram of sugar | 1 gram of fiber

Ambrosia

10 minutes to prepare | 0 minutes to cook | 4 servings 8

3 oranges, quartered and segmented

2 cups diced peaches (4 oz/113 g) in depleted water 1 cup unsweetened coconut that has been crushed

1 compartment (8 ounces/227 g) fat-free a light cream

1. Toss the oranges, peaches, coconut, and crème fraîche together in a large blending bowl. Toss gently until everything is well mixed. Refrigerate for at least 24 hours after covering with plastic wrap.

111 calories per serving | 5 grams of fat | 2 grams of protein | 12 grams of carbohydrates | 8 grams of sugars | 3 grams of fiber

30 minutes to prepare | 20 minutes to cook | 10 servings Pudding:

erythritol (or any sugar substitute): 34 cup 14 teaspoon salt 5 tablespoons almond flour

212 cup milk (non-fat)

6 tbsp. egg substitute, arranged

12 tsp extract de vanille

2 sections (8 oz/227 g) sugar-free squashed spelt hazelnut rolls
5 medium sliced bananas

5 large egg whites Meringue (1 cup)

14 cup erythritol (sugar substitute)

12 tsp extract de vanille

Produce the Pudding

1. Combine the erythritol, almond flour, salt, and milk in a saucepan and whisk to combine. Cook until the sugar is dissolved over medium heat. 2. Whisk together the eggs and cook for about 10 minutes, or until thickened. 3. Remove the vanilla and remove from the heat. 4. Spread the thickened pudding on the bottom of a 3-by-6-inch serving dish. 5. Arrange the squashed rolls on top of the pudding in a layer. 6. On top of the biscuits, layer sliced bananas.

To make the Meringue, combine the ingredients in a mixing bowl and whisk until

1. Preheat oven to 350 degrees Fahrenheit (180 degrees Celsius). 2. In a medium mixing bowl, whisk the egg whites until stiff, about 5 minutes. 3. Continue to beat for about 3 minutes after adding the erythritol and vanilla. 4. On top of the banana

pudding, spread the meringue. 5. Place the goulash dish under the broiler for 7–10 minutes, or until lightly browned on top.

323 calories per serving | 14 grams of fat | 12 grams of protein | 42 grams of carbohydrates | 11 grams of sugar | 3 grams of fiber | 148 milligrams of sodium

Nice Cream Pineapple

10 minutes to prepare | 0 minutes to cook | 4 servings 2 cups pineapple, frozen 6

a cup of PB (no additional sugar, salt, or fat) 12 c. almond milk (unsweetened)

1. Place the frozen pineapple and peanut butter in a blender or food processor and blend until smooth. 2. Stir in the almond milk until it's completely smooth. A smooth paste should emerge as a result.

301 calories per serving | 22 grams of fat | 14 grams of protein | 15 grams of carbohydrates | 8 grams of sugar | 4 grams of fiber

Chapter 12 Staples, Sauces, Dips, and Dressings

Chapter Five

Lime Zinger Dressing

5 minutes to prepare | 0 minutes to cook | Serves 14 cup lime juice, freshly squeezed coconut nectar, 3 tblsp.

12 tsp chia seeds (ground)

12 tbsp mustard (Dijon)

12 tsp cumin powder 14 tsp cinnamon allspice powder

12 tsp. salt from the sea

to taste black pepper, freshly ground 1 tsp (discretionary)

Lime juice, nectar, chia seeds, mustard, cumin, cinnamon, allspice, salt, and pepper should all be blended together in a blender. Blend until the mixture is completely smooth. When you need to thin something out, add some water. Refrigerate for up to a week in a container or other tightly sealed holder.

Serving Size:

52 calories | 1 gram fat | 0 gram protein | 12 gram carbohydrates | 9 gram sugars | 1 gram fiber

Dressing: Avocado Basil

5 minutes to prepare | 0 minutes to cook | Serves 6 34 cup avocado cubes 112 tbsp lemon juice (freshly squeezed)

14 cup stuffed basil leaves (approximately) 14 tsp. sea salt, rounded 12 cup + 1-2 tablespoons water, freshly ground dark pepper, to taste

12 teaspoons coconut nectar or maple syrup, unadulterated

1. Blend the avocado, lemon juice, basil, salt, pepper, 12 cup water, and 1 teaspoon nectar or syrup in a blender until smooth. Puree the mixture until it is silky smooth. If desired, add an additional 1 to 2 tablespoons water and 12 teaspoon of nectar or syrup to thin to the desired consistency. To taste, add a pinch of salt and pepper.

41 calories per serving | 3 grams of fat | 0 grams of protein | 4 grams of carbohydrates | 2 grams of sugars | 1 gram of fiber | 149 milligrams of sodium

Salsa de Ajo

10 minutes to prepare | 0 minutes to cook | 4 servings 4 c. tomatoes, peeled and sliced

13 cup cleaved green onion (14 cup minced onion)

14 cup ringer pepper, minced

1 huge garlic clove, minced or crushed 1 small jalapeo pepper, cultivated and minced

ground lime juice, 1 tablespoon

12 tsp. salt from the sea

12 tsp cumin powder (optional)

1/8 tsp allspice

to taste black pepper, freshly ground

¼ cup minced cilantro (optional) (optional)

1. In an enormous bowl, join the tomatoes, onion, chime pepper, jalapeño pepper, garlic, lime juice, salt, cumin (if utilizing), allspice, dark pepper, and cilantro (if utilizing) (if utilizing). Mix to consolidate. Taste, and add additional salt or flavors as wanted. Serve or refrigerate in an impenetrable compartment until prepared to use (inside 2 to 3 days) (inside 2 to 3 days).

Per Serving\sCalorie: 27 | fat: 0.3g | protein: 1g | carbs: 6g | sugars: 3g | fiber: 2g | sodium: 301mg

Green Chickpea Hummus

5 minutes to prepare | 0 minutes to cook | Serves 6\scups frozen green chickpeas

1 can (15 ounces) white beans, flushed and drained ¼ cup lemon juice 1 huge clove garlic (or more to taste) (or more to taste)   cup new basil leaves

   cup new parsley leaves 1 tablespoon tahini

1 teaspoon ocean salt\s½ teaspoon ground cumin\stablespoons water (optional) (optional) ½ teaspoon lemon zing (optional) (optional)

1. Add the chickpeas to a pot of bubbling water and cook for one moment to draw out their energetic green tone. Eliminate, run under cool water to stop the cooking system, and channel. In a food processor, join the chickpeas, beans, lemon juice, garlic, basil, parsley, tahini, salt, and cumin. Puree until smooth, scratching down the bowl depending on the situation. Add the water whenever wanted to thin or assist the pureeing with handling. Add the lemon zing, whenever wanted, and season to taste. Serve.

Per Serving\sCalorie: 176 | fat: 3g | protein: 10g | carbs: 29g | sugars: 3g | fiber: 8g | sodium: 477mg

Punchy Mustard Vinaigrette

5 minutes to prepare | 0 minutes to cook | 4 servings 6\s¼ cup apple juice vinegar or rice vinegar 2 tablespoons tamari\s1½ tablespoons yellow or Dijon mustard

2½ tablespoons coconut nectar or unadulterated maple syrup

½ tablespoon ground chia

to taste black pepper, freshly ground

⅛ teaspoon ocean salt

1. In a blender, join the vinegar, tamari, mustard, nectar or syrup, chia, pepper, and salt. Puree until completely joined. Taste, and add additional mustard in the event that you love it! Season to taste with extra salt and pepper, whenever wanted. Serve promptly or refrigerate. Dressing will save for no less than seven days in the fridge.

Per Serving\sCalorie: 33 | fat: 0.4g | protein: 1g | carbs: 7g | sugars: 5g | fiber: 1g | sodium: 428mg

Dreamy Caesar Dressing

10 minutes to prepare | 0 minutes to cook | 4 servings 12 ¼⅓ cup drenched almonds or cashews

½ cup cooked red or yellow potato, skins eliminated 2 tablespoons newly crushed lemon juice 1½ tablespoons red wine vinegar

1 medium or huge clove garlic, slashed (conform to taste) (conform to taste) 1 tablespoon chickpea miso (or other gentle enhanced miso) (or other gentle enhanced miso) 2 teaspoons Dijon mustard

12 tsp. salt from the sea

to taste black pepper, freshly ground 1 teaspoon unadulterated maple syrup

¾ cup plain low-fat nondairy milk

2-3 tablespoons water or nondairy milk (optional) (optional)

1. In a blender, consolidate the nuts, potato, lemon juice, vinegar, garlic, miso, mustard, salt, pepper, syrup, and milk. Puree the mixture until it is silky smooth. Add the water or extra milk to thin the dressing, whenever wanted. (It will thicken after refrigeration.)

Serving Size:

Calorie: 34 | fat: 2g | protein: 1g | carbs: 4g | sugars: 1g | fiber: 1g | sodium: 177mg

Fresh Tomato Salsa

Prep time: 10 minutes | Cook time: 0 minutes | Serves 6 2 or 3 medium, ready tomatoes, diced\s½ red onion, minced\sserrano pepper, cultivated and minced Juice of 1 lime\s¼ cup minced new cilantro\s¼ teaspoon salt

1. In a little bowl, join the tomatoes, onion, serrano pepper, lime juice, cilantro, and salt, and blend well. Taste and season with extra salt depending on the situation. 2. Serve promptly, or move to an impermeable holder and refrigerate for up to 3 days.

Per Serving\sCalorie: 18 | fat: 0g | protein: 1g | carbs: 4g | sugars: 1g | fiber: 1g | sodium: 84mg

Caramelized Onion and Greek Yogurt Dip

Prep time: 10 minutes | Cook time: 45 minutes | Serves 8\stablespoons extra-virgin olive oil 3 cups cleaved onions\sgarlic clove, minced\scups plain nonfat Greek yogurt 1 teaspoon salt

black pepper, freshly ground

In a huge pot, heat the olive oil over medium hotness until gleaming. Add the onions, and mix well to cover. Decrease hotness to low, cover, and cook for 45 minutes, blending each the 5 to 10 minutes, until very much sautéed and caramelized. Add the garlic and mix until simply fragrant.

Eliminate from the hotness and let cool for 10 minutes. 3. In a blending bowl, consolidate the onions, yogurt, salt, and pepper.

Serving Size:

Calorie: 83 | fat: 4g | protein: 6g | carbs: 7g | sugars: 5g | fiber: 1g | sodium: 264mg

Oregano Tomato Marinara

Prep time: 5 minutes | Cook time: 15 minutes | Serves 8\s1 (28-ounce/794-g) can entire tomatoes 2 tbsp olive oil (extra virgin)

4 garlic cloves, minced

½ teaspoon salt

¼ teaspoon dried oregano

1. Discard about portion of the fluid from the jar of tomatoes, and move the tomatoes and staying fluid to a huge bowl. Utilize clean hands or a huge spoon to split the tomatoes up. 2. In an enormous skillet, heat the olive oil over medium hotness. Add the garlic and salt, and cook until the garlic simply starts to sizzle, without allowing it to brown. 3. Add the tomatoes and their fluid to the skillet. 4. Stew the sauce for around 15 minutes until the oil starts to isolate and become dim orange and the sauce thickens. Add the oregano, mix, and eliminate from the hotness. 5. After the marinara has cooled to room temperature, store in glass holders in the fridge for up to 3 or 4 days, or in zip-top cooler sacks for up to 4 months.

Per Serving\scalories: 48 | fat: 4g | protein: 1g | carbs: 4g | sugars: 2g | fiber: 1g | sodium: 145mg

Lime Tomato Salsa

Prep time: 10 minutes | Cook time: 0 minutes | Serves 6

2 or 3 medium, ready tomatoes, diced

½ red onion, minced

1 serrano pepper, cultivated and minced Juice of 1 lime

¼ cup minced new cilantro

¼ teaspoon salt

1. In a little bowl, consolidate the tomatoes, onion, serrano pepper, lime juice, cilantro, and salt, and blend well. Taste and season with extra salt on a case by case basis. 2. Serve promptly, or move to a hermetically sealed holder and refrigerate for up to 3 days.

Per Serving

calories: 18 | fat: 0g | protein: 1g | carbs: 4g | sugars: 1g | fiber: 1g | sodium: 84mg

Chapter Six

Conclusion

I have lost north of 6 kg and have a more drawn out history of ordinary blood glucose levels. I have no longing or need to return to my old propensities for unfortunate eating." I might attempt a delectable looking sweet baked good at my cherished bistro down the road and see what occurs. I don't figure a little treat will hurt anybody. That is the edge Type 2 diabetes cookbook for fledglings has over each and every other diabetes cookbook. The opportunity to eat quality food sources while additionally eating the best. Concocting a sound diabetic eating regimen doesn't need to be astounding, and you don't need to relinquish all your beloved food varieties since you're diabetic. The initial step to settling on sound and more astute decisions is to make way of life changes through a solid eating routine, solid living and working out. Similarly as with any smart dieting plan, a diabetic eating regimen is more with regards to the general dietary example rather than fixating on explicit food sources. Follow the 21-day supper plan in this book and eat more normal, natural food and less bundled and helpful food sources to appreciate great health.I have lost north of 6 kg and have a more drawn out history of ordinary blood glucose levels. I have no longing or need to return to my old propensities for unfortunate eating." I might attempt a delectable looking sweet baked good at my cherished bistro down the road and see what occurs. I don't figure a little treat will hurt anybody. That is the edge Type 2 diabetes cookbook for fledglings has over each and every other diabetes cookbook. The opportunity to eat quality food sources while additionally eating the best. Concocting a sound diabetic eating regimen doesn't need to be astounding, and you don't need to relinquish all your beloved food varieties since you're diabetic. The initial step to settling on sound and more astute decisions is to make way of life changes through a solid eating routine, solid living and working out. Similarly as with any smart dieting plan, a diabetic eating regimen is more with regards to the general dietary example rather than fixating on explicit food sources. Follow the 21-day supper plan in this book and eat more normal, natural food and less bundled and helpful food sources to appreciate great health.